We are all born into this world lost, and we seek
our place within it by fashioning a compass out of our
experiences. Bret Shepard's debut collection, *Place Where
Presence Was*, is a smart, intellectual interrogation of the
ontological arguments that exist underneath the surface
of our daily lives. Shepard deconstructs loss and desire
by meditating on the fallibility of memory, the fluidity of
time, and the destruction of the physical landscapes that
we inhabit and share. With a sparse aesthetic, classical
allusions, and sharp intelligence, Shepard's poems explain
how "myth enters the body," and in the face of pain and
loss "life still exists in doses of moments." This book is a
shining example of the mind's ability to triumph.

—John McCarthy,
author of *Scared Violent Like Horses*

What happens when you combine the taut precision of
mathematical equations with the sumptuousness of nude
paintings? In *Place Where Presence Was*, we see poetry
whittled down to its barest core, its round bloody bones,
flavored with subtle humor as they pursue the questions
that define our humanity in the first place.

—Michael Meyerhofer,
author of *Ragged Eden*

A beautiful reflection on the world around as well as the world within, *Place Where Presence Was* draws out the splendor of spaces that often go unnoticed or unspoken. These are the hidden backyard places, the abandoned cars and memories and bodies that are around us every day. Shepard employs form and language that inspire real thought about environments, communities, and selves. This wonderfully intelligent collection of poems offers new ways of seeing the world at a time when we need such perspective more than ever.

—Sarah Nolan,
author of *Unnatural Ecopoetics: Unlikely Spaces in Contemporary Poetry*

"Though I've no exact way to say where I am, which is to say know who I am," Bret Shepard writes, "these words are the only map." In *Place Where Presence Was*, his attempt "to say where" and "to know who" we are, language simultaneously becomes the means of mapping the world and the landscape itself as he adopts the dual role of cartographer and world-builder. His collection is like a globe, both representation and reality, in which each poem is a distinct region encompassed by its opening and closing words. At the same time, the collection's linguistic terrain—concrete yet paradoxical, spare yet stratified—is present in every poem, drawing its own fluid borders with "lines the shape of memory." Shepard stands at the frontier where "words / form our geology," where the body is both position and possibility. Follow him wherever he leads.

—José Edmundo Ocampo Reyes,
author of *Present Values*

Place Where Presence Was

Bret Shepard

MOON CITY PRESS
Department of English
Missouri State University
901 South National Avenue
Springfield, Missouri 65897

The story contained herein is a work of fiction. All incidents, situations, institutions, governments, and people are fictional, and any similarity to characters or persons living or dead is strictly coincidental.

First Edition
Copyright © 2021 by Bret Shepard
All rights reserved.
Published by Moon City Press, Springfield, Missouri, USA, in 2021.

Library of Congress Cataloging-in-Publication Data

Shepard, Bret.
Place where presence was: poems / Bret Shepard.

2021934421

Further Library of Congress information is available upon request.

ISBN-10: 0-913785-59-8
ISBN-13: 978-0-913785-59-1

Cover art: *Place Where Presence Was* by Charli Barnes,
digital mixed media, 5.5 by 8.5 inches, 2020.

Text edited by and copyedited by Karen Craigo.
Cover designed by Charli Barnes.

Author photo by Walter Colley Images.

Manufactured in the United States of America.

www.moon-city-press.com

TABLE OF CONTENTS

II.

III.

For Rebecca

Place
Where
Presence
Was

COMPASSED

Once, the entire world went dark
when the sun set. No one found

other bodies in the night. Everyone
absented touch in winter. This made

December the first metaphor
for death. But not everyone died.

They learned to start fires at night.
Then the moon became the second

metaphor for death, when under it
everyone learned to make love.

I.

NOTE TO SELF

No matter the size of window,
nor the contrary force

with which it resists,
when the window breaks

the outcome is evening.
There is only one method

for self-reflection. To achieve
a quiet mind you must first

hear it speak. Then you must
talk back to your mind

until you talk it to death.

PLACE WHERE PRESENCE WAS

At breakfast I can't eat, so I draw
a topographical map of where

your body was. I look for relief
when you're not here. Contour lines

down your side of the bed, then up
the refrigerator door, its elevation

suggesting your torso, and inside it
the eggs you'd break on yourself.
        Then the dip

in the couch where your body sat
drinking coffee. Dark concentrations

where lines bunch together. Dark
stains on the cushion keeping shape.

OUR CHEMISTRY IS DESIRE

You've stopped listening to wind.
Either way, the trees drop leaf after leaf after leaf.

Anything can drop
under routine circumstances. A leaf. Temperature.
Even your presence in the minds of others can fall.

Not in the way you might think,
as in your memory plummeting into oblivion.
It happens the way tree limbs forget themselves.

LIVING AS MAGNETS

The mood of the oven—
       plastic is more than plastic

when it burns. Did we design this
room to smell of plastic? The open
floor plan circles us into each other.
And who cares.

And who suffocates. Fields suffocate
as snowfall pulls our bodies outside.

It shouldn't be shameful to breathe.

Wheat stubble crunches as feet
sink into snow. The ground pulls us.

For as long as I can remember
the ground has been pulling us,
as if iron laced our bones, promising
       last breaths, a few

last clear breaths.

SAFE DISTANCE

If I said, *Remove weapons
from your bodily calendar,*
I'd not mark my position.
In the horizon, April's
shore waits to be visited.
It is exurban and bright,
a calendar to be marked,
full of things that need
a water supply. I'd bet
limbs that happiness is
the sum of days with X
through them, that time
is only one way to count
the breath of the people
not breathing. Here we are
all approaching the shore
with hands turned inward,
waiting to identify ourselves.

SKIN INTERIM

Hands to map the body—
its landscape, its scarce setting.

Here a valley of freckles, starved.
Here a dimpled rash in morning.

The inability of bodies to respond

to an ecology: touch betrays touch
betrays how we replenish.

Sometimes one of us moves

the other. I've seen a magnet that
resembles the shape of your hand.

PARADE

The rupture
has come

to the city
so I bought it

tickets to view
its constituent

limbs, the bodies
that host them.

Pain is just

another word
for order.

Order is not
an assembly

between edges
of a city. It is

physical pain
inside its

insides as
the bodily

show begins
to culture.

SEASON TURNS CONDITIONAL

West of midwinter, the house holds

the chill. Do you feel how
fragile a foundation, in this city

where concrete is ice, we live on
together. We practice a trade

but goods between two people
make two bodies stale. First work, iron

the clothes we never take off, never
replace with clean. Second work, burn

ideas needing the sun. This season
outside is a concept. Just observe

how light changes. Third work, huddle
our bodies on the dryer as it spins,

shaking our skin into a false friction.

THE UMBRELLA

The woman, not the umbrella,
works the room as a metaphor.

Her nose balances the umbrella
as she eyes the absent man.

It is not a red umbrella, but casts
a red, transparent shadow.

The apparent: she is not alone.
The room is company. She is not

sure what the umbrella offers
under a reflective cover.

These thoughts are not specifically
hers. Neither are they about his

expressions or how he snuffed
the pleasure out of the plusses.

They are not and yet it is. It is
not nothing as the umbrella falls,

definitively slicing the moment.

THE FUNNEL

Fireworks tempt the sky
to empty itself of its stars,

or to respond and embellish
each shimmer shown.

You say *gold* when you mean

light when you see
the future at past speeds.
                Your camera
captured the dream
your hands

                tried to draw
one evening in 2006. The shelf

experiments with holding
utensils you used. You have

a captured picture. It funnels

weather into your mind,
a firm way to transfer silence.
                Pixels combine

to bleed out the past,
lines the shape of memory.

ECO

I.

Money smells us
in this house. Taking
care to not

damage our ecology
with a lacking
economy, we plant

gardens in the house.
Tomato basement. Corn
closets. Cabbage attic.

Eco from the Greek
meaning to manage
one's household.

2.

The architects
of our house-garden,
we set fire to fields.

Our carpets burn.
Pssst.
Your whisper is fire.

This room is for guests.
It's in flames. We would
rebuild if we could.

Red plastic jugs of gas
for us to crawl into
sleep.

SKIN INTERIM

Even left alone, the body tastes
what the earth feels—

the ontology of an economy
turned self.

Our investment is not defined

as the rain into the ground, the ground
as currency. Not hands.

Not tongues. Not stillness of eyes.
It's none of these things.

THE HAWK

The alp at the end of the street

cleaves my thoughts in solitude.
Address after address piles up

in window shades of February
near a concrete riverbank,

where two kingfishers mate
violently, and then abandon

the desire. Watching, I know
we are more than numbers,

the necessary ways we quiet
into nothing at all, and then

never more absent our sounds.
The street stretches us beyond

the comfort of new asphalt,
where closer to the alp a hawk

on the ground, half a squirrel
in its throat, choked to death.

BACKYARD ORCHARD

Near the coast, field workers
toss peaches into transport bins.

Those peaches are not theirs,
yet they pick them. Peaches

the color of your hair.
Peaches cupped in my hands.
Removing pits,

we decide to landscape
ourselves. Labor and fruit come

out of my mouth. You say *stop
spitting your language at me.*

COMPASS

My arms rest on the rotten pine stump in my backyard. The rain, again, and thunder in the distance—my feet wedge into the mud, hoodie clinging to my skin. I remove it and all my clothes. What am I here? Absent of anyone else, I must question how I know the material world. If the only thing I ever touch again is in this yard, I must question the nature of living. Though I've no exact way to say where I am, which is to say know who I am, these words are the only map. To know this place, which is to say to know me, which is to say know anyone, these materials must be stripped of their vocabulary only to be reassembled by you and me together. True, this will be something similar to impossible. True, each thing exists in itself. True, the rain keeps streaming from the sky, keeps soaking into the ground, and keeps transpiring only to fall once more. That's the trouble. Following a negative compass toward the untrue, which is to say toward the possible, I can see the ground retreating behind clouds. I feel the trees flicker, taste the grasses shaking.

WATER RAINING

In our backyard the window-view slides
from green to smeared translucent

too quickly today. Storm entering
the house, water drifting over shoes—

we fasten senses, prune our bodies,
and nail plywood over our eyes.

Eyes go wooden. No young
garden growth to see. Storms allow

mouths to batten mouths.
To be secured by skin. To be dried clean.

WEATHER

There was a We in weather. We
drifted river-water,

its texture at noon. At—

such a strange hinge,
                           rarely accurate.

According to meteorologists, weather
attains agency in the happening.

We listened from the end of the river.
Trees on the banks continued to panic.

Where were we at? At home.

There was a Her.
                   Now it's unclear where
that refers to. Someone
will boat at that river

in different conditions.
Weather will happen.

SKIN INTERIM

Observe walls: percussed voices
in every room of the house

and bodies like trees. The rooms
whisper that we are fields of skin.

It's all they ever whisper to us.

The mouth of a house
carved into the ceiling of a house

reveals many things—we breathe
animal into animal.

I CAN'T BELIEVE YOU'RE IN LOVE WITH THAT

Musical weather and skin cramps
everyone's style,

the barrier between. Between
me and you. The stereo cringes

its tune through the room and you
sing back to the voice.

For example, take me.

Coffee, please. Two chairs not empty
like two chairs empty. You tell me

I'll understand. My hand runs across
the lacquered tabletop. Its print fades

so slowly I watch the whole of it.

It's been a while. Think about math
from calculus. That long.

Description, you say, is inaccurate.
Your hair looks exactly

like the remains of the past
I buried. Rot. Your face becomes

that other person's problem to devote.
I sit at the table and want

to believe you're here. Disgust in
company kept. Take me, for example.

AESTHETICS

Morning light, the left hand
slowly traces the right
hand as it covers
both my eyes.

MAP OF A SHAPE

A maple tree sways.
Whatever it is it is

magnetic in the way
the maple meets

my eyes halfway
toward sky. I stand

underneath a cloud
resembling the way

I recall your body.

MAGNETIC SENSE

Sun affixed upon a field-bed, you lie
on a sheet in the middle of a hayfield

spread out and damp from the dew.
You keep your focus on the trouble

with the spaces between what matters.
A compass—our cells do experience

magnetic stimulation—where is that
field—yet the body is never enough.

A COMPASS

The sinkhole at the edge of the wheat field,
deepening, a magnet in its center—

it is common to mistake types of birds,
or grasses. I once mistook the trees

for desire. Then, the other day I could not
remember the name of my mother's cancer.

SKIN INTERIM

Abandoned, the body
turns itself, is thirsty
for its life, and more.

In the thickest hours,
to what will the body
commit to knowing?

OTHER CALIFORNIA

Say you're not one of those
lost people in concrete lots

near Malibu and Zuma—
the ocean in your eyes

waves goodbye to the beach
restaurants where you

never ate rockfish tacos—
admit you've not felt the sting
late fall in Santa Ana winds

as heat blows deep through
the mind—a dry riverbed
under California's lights.

For you never swam your life
and the water never was—

and the water was never
the color you swam it.

LOS ANGELES

I was wrong to believe in planning, its false vision
    beneath shirt pockets. Morning's chores,
writing and cooking, bring desperate hunger
    that freshens breakfast; the eggs taste more
like grease from the bacon, the pan still scorched.
    After art, rush hour is more bearable at 8 a.m.
The freeway full of status: car loans and vanity
    plates. Traffic. Accident. Traffic. Police.
A white-tailed deer, cousin of the circumpolar
    caribou, meanders across the 101 freeway
down from the West Hollywood Hills. Its antlers
    and that I'm digesting a settler's breakfast
means this should be Alaska. Instead,
    industry wakes up. If I hear one more car horn,
one more set of screeching tires, one more siren—
    I've been thinking about thinking about
last love, but I start remembering too much.
    Out bad sides. Out patchy dreams. Endurance.
It's to the point where all there is to do is circles
    never running into something concrete. I'm there,
an in-state, never crossing the border.

WE ARE NOT THE SUM OF OUR ACTIONS

The rust-marooned Chevy sits in the ditch.
After decades of this it offers nothing more
than a plug slowing the creek's abrasion of land.
Deployed by a farmhand into moist sediment
some spring morning, grazing fields hold it
close, a forced embrace.

I want to imagine it was placed by accident.
Maybe the night was deep. Maybe the drinks
did the driving. Maybe the farmhand was
angry with life, the wife he married fast,
his share of crops unimagined that harvest,
debt mounted to his name, claiming his job.

It could have been all that, but it was not.
Practicality pushed the car into the earth,
the only thing that drove us in those days.

WEST ENDING

Enter bullet. This existence beaten
from memory, maybe I should take two

camera shots to preserve tracks.
Before. After. Maybe pave me. Three

loggers told me a chainsaw's story,
a valid way of hearing the wild.

Three radicals exploded machinery.
Eleven are in pieces with belief. Five

inner-city shootings might compare
favorably with what we nightmare.

That from a priest who missions
in villages where people consider seven

ideas their only vexation. I believe belief.
The way it ruins the ending. *Exit bullet.*

A NOTE ON BEGINNINGS

Cylinder repeats. Ammo and quick release caliber
noise the air. We understand because of the names—

trigger, barrel, hammer—the utility of a gun's steel form—
precision, loading—pace in an automatic world.

Powerful documents—the scripture of bloodshed,
the past that is our foundation.

Bullet shells fall behind—
the inhalation of bitter imprints

human texture. It is the piercing—sound—impact—
that registers. Spring-propelled motion,

like our world's tilted axis—
with every trigger-pull we see through life, the machine.

SKIN INTERIM

When used recklessly, words may be dropped
onto our fingers. To prevent future damage

we bandage our mouths thick with gauze.

After years of repeating the same phrase
we now understand the subtext. We unplant

the bird, the body, the youth—what we buried

becomes understood again in physical form.
This must be what we intended—action

unearthed after speech. Strike me. Hold me.

EXPANDING WITNESS

He burns the skin off their legs
to make them walk, make them alive, their deprived

metatarsals—skeletal as a map, its barbed lines.

Witness to removal—hands to fan the flame,
the smell of rotten veins, their exposure to lighter fluid

perceptions—the charred carcasses
puddle the margins of gravel. He grips

one hand on hock, fetlock resting on knee.

Repeating landscape, each skeleton forms a field.
There is so much life in bones—his motive and motion to

burn the sickness—how he unravels the skein of stillness,
animating the dead, their count rising as integer tinder.

Legs expand and then contract with pressure.
For days he returns to delete the bones, their traces,

how he buries life in his stomach, marrow and all.

DETAILS OF AIR

This, too, to consider during dusk
before the brushfire-warmth

comfort—details of the beach,
flimsy air stutters messages

from one part of the body

to the next part, fingers to chest,
for example, so quickly it might

be called a stuttering of the body—
after enough of us, even this beach

will erode into nothing we can use.

OF PUBLIC

Gunmetal gray walls
lean at angles

into the sky in order
to form the sky.

I'm waiting in Union
Square Station

this morning
to leave this city

to its violence. I have
unwittingly starved

my empty apartment,
the generous view,

the promise to build

against the noise.
I've heard the train

coming, seen its lights
down the tunnel

for as long as it takes
myself to wonder

about jumping into
myself once again.

ARCTIC INTERPRETING

This is to say the language of the Inupiaq,
to recall a way back to the silent earth,

where slow waters run land, cold mapping
        the direction. This is north, there south.
To taste that place,

        where braided streams feed people,
        where ice and ocean fracture boats,

where bone and slate become the ulu.
                To say craft—
        to know the ulu's essence—
      to grip its blade and slice

           the thickest muktuk,
        the most tender eider,
      their meat over wild berries
when summer arrives—

somewhere near the Meade River. To listen
        to the flat land, the chill echoing
the tundra in the Brooks Range.

To wade through ice-melt water. To let oil
collect and reflect. To see it spread.

WORDS FOR SNOW

A language built in silence, when I say snow
I mean to say the spirit of winter, isolation

for isolated minds in the naked freeze—tundra,
permafrost quieting the moss and lichen—

or below the tree line, how alpines slope south
blanketed by a mantle of slush slow to melt.

I say snowfall so lonely that if I could help it
keep falling, perpetual descent in wind's savage

December pulse, if I could help it I would
fall along with it and let winter speak for itself.

SKIN INTERIM

The neighborhood consumed something
of our house. Then our house

consumed everything itself.
Throughout night and into morning

we buried our bodies

under fabric, escaping
to the blurred horizon

beyond yards and fences.
We've already burned the map to guide us

MALIBU, FEBRUARY

Into sun. Out of body.
Views are louder, more

stiff the morning after
martinis. Easy does it

with attitude. Enough

water pools the body
& memory takes a dip.

Easy walks in & out
of the hot tub to theorize

feminine/masculine.

To drain the pool,
chemical traces, skin

refuses to burn, sun

on the eyes. We have
the eyes for looking

at nothing serious
for far, far too long.

DESIRE SWELLS

The sea declares such a volume to body
shore, before you see whitecaps cresting

like a mouth as it breaks into you. You see
the edges of what it is
                              to desire
                                        desire,

a careful shade of eyes,
the curve of bone casting
                              a shadow, swells

to embrace you and then
                              embracing you

reach an inevitable and complete collapse
unseen in a privacy,
                         in such a brutal privacy.

THE TROUBLE

I.

Memory creates impossible versions.

2.

The old stories: a clay lover
cannot cross water. A lover made of iron
cannot move through a furnace.

A wooden lover cannot pass through fire
to run back from the wild and find us.
We cannot build a life with desire.

3.

We don't write the enviable into life.
We don't awaken a fire from sleep.

There are promises and wishes
no one makes simultaneously.

4.

If we could butcher desire into parts,
the things we could have built here.

RE-PLACED

I looked hard
for the Atlantic.

I'm at the edge
of myself

in Nebraska
and so found

the Missouri
River. It pales.

It interrupts
and is edged
by fields.

I am like that
in that

I am like
the field,

lost to lists.

Whatever
the field is

is replaced
with fog.

NEGATIVE COMPASS

Direction is silence beyond the gated forest
edging the field. We gate tonight. Then stop.

Or silence the meadow.
Then stop talking. Or unrest our legs and set ourselves

a path along the creekbed.
Then digest the matter of silence and the voles.

Pace slows the slow of speech, as in words
form our geology.

Then natural matter is as constructed as the rest.
Or we are mountains

peeking above clouds and we smell the fragrance
of biology. Then insect chords make us dance.

Or we erupt.
Then night erupts. Then silence is direction.

II.

PLAY AT BEING PEOPLE

In a fogged-up mirror, you see a glint of metal dripping fluid from its end point. A woman flicks the middle of the metal. She is wearing the metal as lingerie. You're a monster, she says. You're becoming a monster. And then the lights flicker rapidly like eyes blinking when an eyelash gets lost behind the lid. If you look over to the light switch, a set of fingers is visible. You might think it's a trick, but it isn't. Those fingers have nothing to do with the light source's instability. A little higher than the fingers is a set of eyes, your eyes. And you see yourself watching her as she transforms into something different, something she calls a monster. Soon the distance between you and her reduces to the point of obscurity. There is no you. There is no her, only a conglomerate body. It, which was once she and you, has become the monster you always knew existed somewhere in this house.

In her backyard, palmettos
sound too precious to be

covered in fluid. The birthday
party is over, bodies no longer

singing. She drops
the point

of the umbrella
into a balloon,
thus popping it.

The magnetic fluid retains
some of its virtue even

after being extracted
from the body, not unlike

the sound of the flute
that loses itself by degrees.

She desires danger
so she raffles her stomach off
to the weakest branch.

One morning, at such a time that it could still be considered night, she calls an ambulance. She tells herself that Western medicine answers her skin. The medicine strewn on the table enlivens the room. It animates the empty space. Whether it's night or morning only matters if you visualize her body in that room. As she drops each pill into glasses of water, the pills bloom into varieties of birds. The diazepam becomes a blue jay. Some starlings appear. Then a crow. Two cardinals in the place of morphine pills. Myth enters the body. She cancels the ambulance. Life still exists in doses of moments. The birds come together in the center of the room, hover around her nakedness, and then lift her body closer and closer to the ceiling fan made of rotating clouds.

You watch as she scoops a palm's worth of dirt
from the river—the coarseness scraping

against a migration of harmful fluids
stolen into the body. Mesmerized—

corrupted soil on the tongue. Birds tip over
the feeder hanging from the palmetto's

fractured limb. The branches break
themselves. The body also breaks

when confronting the unknown rooms.
Every thing in nature has

a communication by an universal fluid,
in which all bodies are plunged. Each path

leads up and onto the uncivilized branches,
as in someone climbing against you.

The field needs to be dressed nicely for harvest. It needs to shed summer's color. Confusing red, so many shades. Think of blood, that darker shade. Think of sunset, that dying shade. Locate the difference between alone and empty. Sometime, just reach your hand into there.

The body needs to be touched if one is to remove harmful fluids. Franz Mesmer called it animal magnetism. *Touching is applied to the principal organs, the breast, the stomach, and chiefly the place called the hollow.* The trouble is here and here and here.

BOILING SAND

Forty gone down together
Into the boiling sand.
Ring, for the scant salvation!

—Emily Dickinson

1.

A string of motion, unplanned
particles streamed all at once

into boil. At the beach,
lost voices eddied near shore,

turned each of our heads
long enough to see our home

entering every flame we ever lit.

2.

To add *ex-* to anything is violent. To X out.

Dancing on the rooftop, you shouted at me
to bring the Anchor Steam and a lighter.

We watched the beach liquefy in places
we walked, sand exploding in steps. Memory

to wipe the X away like ash. Then, to re-see—
first sand, and then fire, and then the boiling.

3.

In defiance, the earthquake departed clothes.

Isn't that why we shared laundry, so as to identify,
to smell like each other, to know who belongs

and who is a monster, unwelcome in the darkness,
as if the ocean needs no identification to enter it,

as if we danced on rooftops with enough intensity
the explosions of life would repeal into touch.

4.

Remember home. Flooded bedrooms, too.
The abstract boils into the specific. Water

sneaks up to a beach and the driftwood
reclaims itself for itself. Coral sand

gestures to what we can't see, that we know

so little of life. Glass sand is trace
to garbage, that it reflects so much of us.

5.

Remember our peeling faces from the ocean,

the tide like undressing
small surprises in the window, so many waves

full of sand turning over silt, a destruction
of uncorked eyes, a desirous look or two.

Touch, a sail. You said to be amazed
even by moments we intend to have happen.

6.

Edges of life on Black Sands Beach
tethered the noise from your voice

streaming. Words like vapor steamed

the cove. Isn't that why we posed bodies
into photos, so as to bribe the future.

We can be disappointed even
by moments we want to be amazing.

7.

There was no pier. To say what something is
acknowledges it is nothing and everything.

Sand attacks from two sides, into all places.
There was no beach party. In shallow depths

water and sand liquefy to anticipate
being shaken. I'm not saying one of us was sand,

the other water. It is a fact that goes unspoken.

8.

To identify when nothing is everything—
the monster in the closet loved to whisper

to the monster under the bed. *Sink the bed.*

We looked before sleep and saw nothing,
heard everything. The shadows hummed

forty versions of a song scared into distance,
not like how a beach fire might scorch flesh.

9.

Should music proceed from darkness
when every beach is home to a midnight

of thoughts. I took your missing bags
to mean you caught the coastal train,

the narrow chill when tracks opened
memories like veins. Thinking now,

I park between moments of sunlight.

10.

I parked myself on the boiling sand
below midnight, talking to social media.

I saw pictures posted. You, already gone.

I took your new clothes to mean fire
caught the first ticket to summer

after it swept through downtown,
the only bar we liked in whisky flames.

11.

The train. My window. Metal
on metal. Sand on sand.

The radio, home leaning
on the breaks and into error.

How can I wave a memory
into ocean, the thick silence

between on and off some track.

12.

First flesh, then heat, and then the boiling.
Sometimes an ingredient stays nothing

but individual, a life already beyond itself.
Something about its chemistry. Something, too,

in embrace, in the sand, and then in the fire.

In our swims for wisdom, we found we must
reach the shore before the monster sinks us.

13. —*Laura Jenson*

But the bad boats are ready to be bad,
to overturn in water, to demolish the swagger

and the sway. To be guideless in the tide
at night, that is true death. *They are bad boats*

because they cannot wind their own rope
or guide themselves neatly close to the wharf.

How do we get back on track if there is only water.

14. —*Samuel Green*

Listen: the ground takes everything
that comes. Everything. So does the water

if you listen at night, as someone enters the tide.
First solitude, then fear, and then the desire

to landscape the bed. *Too much drought*
in too many hearts. But I remember drowning

as any part of California widening into our mouths.

15.

Next to my lost presence in bed,
an elephant rests, my voice built

into its chest. The elephant sleeps
with you, but not without people

like you. There is static difference,

like who asked to heat your body
or anyone else's body into a boil.

16.

We tried to boil water between two cities,
left it burning to carry waves.

No matter the time of day, shrimp
eyes into crab eyes into a rope

of pearls, a brief look to stretch screams

into temperature, the silence too
torrential to welcome the fragile answers.

17.

The brim of a sail too loose, and then not
in the distance of a boat, water cuts.

Over the edge we found a sharper edge.

The weekend trips to restart us, episodes
buffering into picture. Always in a hotel

you can find a monster leaving the closet
to enter another monster under the bed.

18.

The water problem constitutes beauty
from abandonment. In us an electric charge

revealed Point Bonita Lighthouse. My body
as a trampoline returning moments in waves.

In a hotel, only negative reality approaches
an escape from one another. Trip Advisor

incorrectly stated the available amenities.

19.

Circularity of time before thoughts boil into water,
memories float themselves like a palette

of rooms. If there are two types of distance,
physical and mental, what do you call the room

between them. It confesses lilies every morning.
It curdles voices into pools we enter naked.

I call it the middle of a cloud moving into horizon.

20.

Bloom of iron in the water. Photos

kept shape of what was trapped
and disappeared before forming

a complete moment. Wheels of sand
sliding the house, a flood so close

to one garment you might have
worn for some anniversary.

21.

What breathing from the heart of the public
outside. What riots in the sudden odor

of your news somewhere else,
another city. I listen for your disturbances

for minutes, hours, nights. I tie myself

to the bedpost to keep listening
hard for your entrance through those walls.

22.

A train of waves the walls can't stop, music
fencing the air along forty rooftops.

If immanence is a physical state we lack,

the act of memory ignites the body's heat.
And if that is not the case, in what respect

does the face react to the closed eyes
across the ocean of sounds to someone else.

23.

It terrifies me to dream of falling into the ocean
without you, or vice versa, a reflection attenuated

as a tire swing fallen into the boiling sand.
To speak of such aggression weaves scarcity

into the vulgar waves. When one of us liberates
the present moment, the monster fear of it,

I think of sailing the tide backward to you.

24.   .

If human beauty is capacity exceeded by event,
isn't that why we continue steal each other's

scents, to memorize our sense of each other,
to think ourselves back to bodies. The bedroom

drifts with waves, the edges having burned
any shore it touched. I tie myself to the bed frame

to depart as the tide leaves and keeps leaving.

Acknowledgments

The following poems have been published, sometimes in different versions, by the following journals. Thanks to the editors and readers of each publication.

American Letters and Commentary, "Negative Compass"; *Arts & Letters*, "The Trouble" and "Desire Swells"; *Boston Review*, "Parade"; *Colorado Review*, "Compassed," "Note to Self," and "Our Chemistry Is Desire"; *Cold Mountain Review*, "West Ending"; *Concho River Review*, "We Are Not the Sum of Our Actions"; *Copper Nickel*, "Los Angeles"; *Crazyhorse*, "Safe Distance"; *Diagram*, "Skin Interim" (as "Skin Interims," including "Even left alone, the body tastes," "Observe walls: percussed voices," "Hands to map the body—," and "The neighborhood consumed something"); *DMQ Review*, "The Umbrella"; *Field*, "Living as Magnets"; *Gravel*, "The Hawk," "A Compass," and "Magnetic Sense"; *Hobble Creek Review*, "Arctic Interpreting"; *Ilk*, from "Play at Being": "In a fogged-up mirror is a glint ...," "One morning, at such a time ...," and "Where it rains, the potential to pour exists"; *Isthmus*, "Details of Air" and "Of Public"; *Leveler*, "Words for Snow"; *Matter*, "A Note on Beginnings" (as "Revolver"); *Pank*, "Place Where Presence Was"; *Permafrost*, "Backyard Orchard" and "Malibu, February"; *Requited*, "Expanding Witness" and "Other California"; *Shampoo*, "Weather"; *Sink Review*, "I Can't Believe You're in Love With That" and "The Funnel"; *Sugar House Review*, "Re-Placed"; *UCity Review*, "Eco" and "Water Raining"; *Whiskey Island*, "Season Turns Conditional."

Poems from this manuscript also appeared in a chapbook, *Negative Compass*, which won the Wells College Chapbook

Prize.

Part II of the manuscript takes language from M. Caullet de Veaumore's Mesmer's *Aphorisms and Instructions*.

I would like to thank my wife, Rebecca. Her generosity and partnership are beyond measure. Thanks to our sons for their energy and laughing alongside of ours. They are the most amazing kids. Thanks to my mother, Linda Shepard, for her unending encouragement and support. She is everything good. And thanks to my brother, Derek Shepard, for showing such care and passion toward life. His interests in ideas and words have always inspired me.

Thanks to Stephen Behrendt, a mentor and a friend. His belief in my work has made all the difference. Many, many thanks to my family, friends, colleagues, and teachers, especially Ryan Aiello, Jeff Alessandrelli, Karen Babine, Rick Barot, Grace Bauer, Mike Benveniste, Chris Burton, Cris Davenport, Graham Foust, Blaine Golden, Brenda Hillman, Jeff Jones, Nima Najafi Kianfar, Kelly Meyer, Jane Miller, Trey Moody, Ashur and Elaine Mooshiabad, Rusty Morrison, Jodie Nicotra, Daniel Orozco, Spencer Pope, Alison Pope, Dan Rosenberg, Scott Slovic, Joshua Ware, Morgan White, and Gary Williams. And many thanks to my peers at Nebraska and Saint Mary's, whose words and community have been vital to my work.

My enormous gratitude goes to Karen Craigo and Michael Czyzniejewski for selecting and believing in this manuscript.

Winners of the Moon City Poetry Award

2014
Sarah Freligh *Sad Math*

2015
Jeannine Hall Gailey *Field Guide to the End of the World*

2016
Kerri French *Every Room in the Body*

2017
Clayton Adam Clark *Finitude of Skin*

2018
Kathy Goodkin *Crybaby Bridge*

2019
Bret Shepard *Place Where Presence Was*

CPSIA information can be obtained
at www.ICGtesting.com
Printed in the USA
FSHW010716080421